AWESOME VALUES IN FAMOUS LIVES

Michael J. Fox

Courage for Life

Barbara Kramer

Enslow Elementary

an imprint of

Enslow Publishers, Inc.

40 Industrial Road	PO Box 38
Box 398	Aldershot
Berkeley Heights, NJ 07922	Hants GU12 6BP
USA	UK

http://www.enslow.com

Enslow Elementary, an imprint of Enslow Publishers, Inc.

Enslow Elementary® is a registered trademark of Enslow Publishers, Inc.

Library of Congress Cataloging-in-Publication Data

Kramer, Barbara.
    Michael J. Fox : courage for life / Barbara Kramer.
           p. cm. — (Awesome values in famous lives)
    Includes bibliographical references and index.
    ISBN-10: 0-7660-2376-1 (hardcover)
    1. Fox, Michael J., 1961–   2. Actors—Canada—Biography—Juvenile literature. 3. Parkinson's disease—
Patients—United States—Biography—Juvenile literature. I. Title.
PN2308.F69K73 2004
791.4302'8'092—dc22

                                          2004004504

ISBN-13: 978-0-7660-2376-5

Printed in the United States of America

10 9 8 7 6 5 4 3

To Our Readers: We have done our best to make sure all Internet Addresses in this book were active and appropriate when we went to press. However, the author and the publisher have no control over and assume no liability for the material available on those Internet sites or on other Web sites they may link to. Any comments or suggestions can be sent by e-mail to comments@enslow.com or to the address on the back cover.

Every effort has been made to locate all copyright holders of material used in this book. If any errors or omissions have occurred, corrections will be made in future editions of this book.

Contents

Michael J. Fox
makes comedy
seem so easy
and natural.

CHAPTER 1

Too Small for Hockey

Michael J. Fox tilts his head to one side, grins, and then waits for a second before he speaks. Michael is an expert at being funny. When he says his line at just the right moment, the audience at the taping of *Spin City* howls with laughter.

Michael loves to make people laugh. Starring in two popular television shows won him millions of fans. His three *Back to the Future* films made him a superstar. But Michael is also battling a very serious illness. In 1998, he told his fans that he had Parkinson's disease.

Michael's family moved to Burnaby, Canada when he was ten.

One sign of Parkinson's is shaking that a person cannot control. Other signs are stiff muscles and problems walking. There is no cure for this sickness. But Michael has found the courage to be happy in spite of his illness. He is also helping other people who have Parkinson's.

Michael was born on June 9, 1961, in Edmonton, Alberta, Canada. He was the second youngest child in a family with two boys and three girls.

His father, William, was an officer in the Canadian army, so the family moved often from one army base to another. Michael never had any trouble making friends. "We'd be in a new city only about a week and people would already know me," he said.[1]

When Michael was not busy with his friends, he might be speeding off on his bike. He also hunted bullfrogs, using a large fishing net to snag them. In quieter times, he liked to read, draw, and write his own stories.

Michael was small for his age. Other kids teased him about being short, but Michael did not let it

A Bright Future

One day, Michael's grandmother made a prediction about his future. "He'll be famous some day," she said.[2] People who knew Michael found that hard to believe. After all, he was only six years old at the time.

bother him. "He always looked on the bright side of things," his mother, Phyllis, said.[3] He was so funny that the bullies started laughing at his jokes instead of making fun of him.

Michael's father retired from the army in 1971. The family settled in the town of Burnaby, near Vancouver in Canada. Ten-year-old Michael loved ice hockey. He imagined playing on a professional team one day.

Michael was very active, and he had a habit of getting hurt. Over the years, he got more than fifty stitches on his face. Some of the cuts came from hockey. Others were from accidents, such as the time he fell out of a bunk bed.

When Michael was fourteen, he gave up his dream of playing in the

Michael had fun acting in school plays
at Burnaby Central High School.

National Hockey League. The other kids were growing bigger, but Michael was still short.

Michael became interested in music. He learned to play the guitar and started a rock band with some friends. They played at high school dances and other places around town.

Michael also signed up for an acting class. Learning lines was easy for him, and he liked making people in the audience laugh.[4] One day, the teacher

Michael's high school picture.

"We'd be in a new city only about a week and people would already know me."

urged him to try out for a part on television. The Canadian Broadcasting Company (CBC) was looking for a ten- to twelve-year-old actor to star in a new comedy show.

Michael was sixteen, but his small size and big talent paid off. He was cast in *Leo and Me* as a ten-year-old orphan who lives with his uncle Leo. Michael worked on the show for two years.

At the same time, he had other acting jobs, too. He landed a part in *Letters from Frank*, an American television movie filmed in Canada. During his last year of high school, in 1978, Michael was in a play called *The Shadow Box*. Acting in the play at night kept him out late. He was often too tired to wake up in the morning. He missed so many days of school that he was failing his classes, even the acting class.

Michael talked to his parents about his future. Could he quit school to become an actor? His parents were not pleased, but they did not stop him.

A few months later, Michael left Canada. He moved to southern California to try to get into the movie business. He was eighteen years old and on his own in a new country.

CHAPTER 2

Rising Star

Michael's first acting job in the United States was a small part in the teen movie *Midnight Madness*. Next, he beat out more than three hundred other actors to win a role in a new CBS television series, *Palmerstown USA*. It was on TV in 1980 and 1981. Michael also appeared in some popular 1980s TV shows, such as *Trapper John, M.D.*,

The Love Boat, and *Lou Grant*. He had a small part in *Class of 1984*, a movie about teenagers in a high school.

After these jobs, Michael had no work for a while. He was trying out for plenty of parts, but he was not having any luck. That happens to many actors, but Michael had not saved up for the slow times. He had spent his money as fast as he

Michael added a "J" to his name when he learned that there was another actor named Michael Fox.

earned it. "I was an idiot," he said.[1] How would he pay all his bills?

Michael was broke. He sold his car, moved into a smaller apartment, and started selling his furniture, piece by piece. After a few months, he was ready to give up and go back to Canada.

Just in time, Michael heard about a new television series that needed a teen actor. Michael was twenty-one years old, but he looked much younger. He was chosen to play fifteen-year-old Alex Keaton on *Family Ties*. The first show was on television in September 1982.

Family Ties was a comedy about a family with three children— two girls and one boy.

Michael seemed calm and sure of himself, but he was really nervous at first on *Family Ties*.

The cast of *Family Ties*, clockwise from top:
Michael Gross (dad), Justine Bateman, Tina Yothers,
Michael J. Fox, and Meredith Baxter Birney (mom).

The boy, Alex, was very different from the rest of the family. The parents on the show cared about world peace and saving the environment. Alex's only interest was making money. He liked to wear a tie to school and act like a businessman.

Alex could be bossy and selfish, but he was lovable, too. Michael was the perfect actor for the part. He made Alex Keaton seem funny and cute, even when he was arguing with his family. Before long, he was the most popular actor on the show.

When Michael was not busy with *Family Ties*, he worked on other acting jobs. He starred in two television movies: *High School U.S.A.* and *Poison Ivy*. In another movie, *Teen Wolf*, he was a high school student who turns into a basketball-playing werewolf.

In *Back to the Future*, Michael starred with Christopher Lloyd, far right. Playing Marty McFly made Michael a superstar.

Then, in 1985, Michael was asked to star in a movie called *Back to the Future*. It is a comedy about a skateboarding teenager who travels back in time to the 1950s. Michael was excited about being in this movie. But it was being filmed at the same time as *Family Ties*. Could he do both?

For three months, Michael worked day and night. He acted in *Family Ties* during the day, then rushed to the movie set. *Back to the Future* kept him busy for half the night. After a few hours of sleep, it was time for *Family Ties* again. Michael was worn out, but his hard work made him a big star.

Back to the Future was the most popular film in the United States in the summer of 1985.

As the star of *Family Ties*, Michael received as many as 21,000 fan letters each week.

The second most popular film was *Teen Wolf*.

During the 1985–1986 season of *Family Ties*, a new character joined the show. Actress Tracy Pollan played the role of Alex's first girlfriend. By that time, *Family Ties* was a huge hit.

Now that Michael was rich and famous, he bought a house with a swimming pool. He filled his garage with fancy cars. In his rare moments of free time, Michael liked to watch sports on television. Ice hockey was his favorite. But mostly Michael was too busy with his TV show and making movies.

Michael and Tracy Pollan became friends on the set of *Family Ties*.

CHAPTER 3

Back to the Future–Again

Michael was working at a dizzying speed. He finished the fourth season of *Family Ties* in March 1986. The next day he flew to Chicago to begin filming *Light of Day*. In this drama, Michael plays a guitarist in a small band.

When he was done with the movie in May, he headed straight to New York to star in a comedy, *The Secret of My Success*. He played a country farm boy who lands a job in New York City. Just one day after finishing this movie, Michael was back in California to tape another season of *Family Ties*.

Although Tracy Pollan was no longer in *Family Ties*, she and Michael soon had another chance to work together. Both were cast in *Bright Lights, Big City*, a film based on a best-selling book. On the set of this movie, Michael and Tracy fell in love.

On July 16, 1988, they were married at a small hotel in Arlington, Vermont. They wanted a private wedding and tried to keep their plans secret. They did not succeed. Helicopters circled overhead with

And the Winner Is . . .

Everyone loved Michael in *Family Ties*, and he won three Emmy awards for the show. He was named Best Actor in a Comedy Series in 1986, 1987, and 1988.

Michael and Tracy in 2000. Tracy, too, appears in plays, movies, and television shows.

photographers trying to snap pictures. "It was nuts," said Michael.[1]

In his next movie, *Casualties of War*, Michael played a soldier in the Vietnam War. People who saw the movie liked Michael's acting, but *Casualties of War* did not make a lot of money. None of Michael's serious films were as popular as his comedies. It seemed that his fans wanted him to be funny.

In 1989, Michael was racing back and forth to do *Family Ties* and *Back to the Future II* at the same time. In *Back to the Future II*, Michael's character, Marty McFly, blasted into the future to the year 2015.

After being on television for seven years, *Family Ties* ended in 1989. For Michael, it was an important year for another reason, too—the birth of his son, Samuel. Michael was thrilled to be a dad.

Michael had to finish one more *Back to the Future* movie before he could take a vacation with his wife and son. In *Back to the Future III*, he traveled back

A Stunt Gone Wrong

Michael did many of his own movie stunts. In *Back to the Future III*, the villain hangs Marty McFly by a rope around his neck. Everybody on the set thought Michael was doing a great acting job. It all looked very real. Then Michael passed out, and they discovered that his "struggling" was not an act—it was real. Something had gone wrong with the stunt, and the rope was getting too tight on Michael's neck. Luckily, a doctor on the set rushed to help Michael.

to the Old West of 1885. After that, Michael was ready for a break. The Fox family enjoyed some peace and quiet at their vacation home, a big farm in Vermont.

Soon Michael was back in New York City playing a Hollywood actor in *The Hard Way*. This movie did poorly at the movie theaters. Michael's fans were happier with *Doc Hollywood*, in which he played a city doctor who gets stuck in a small country town.

It was in Florida, during the filming of *Doc Hollywood*, that Michael noticed something odd. The pinky finger of his left hand kept twitching. Within six months, other fingers were twitching, too. His hand felt weak, and his left shoulder was stiff. It took many tests to finally find the cause.

In 1991, the doctors gave Michael some bad news. He had Parkinson's disease.

When he was making the movie
Doc Hollywood, Michael knew that something
was wrong with him—but what was it?

CHAPTER 4

A Huge Secret

Michael was shocked. He was thirty years old. Parkinson's usually strikes people over sixty. His life had been going so well. What would happen now? Some people with Parkinson's cannot walk, talk, or take care of themselves. Michael was scared and upset.

A movie star's fans want to know everything about him. If news of Michael's illness got out, reporters would be knocking at his door. They would ask hard questions: How would Parkinson's change his life? Would he be able to make more movies?

Michael needed time to learn more about the disease. He decided to keep the news secret. He and Tracy told only their families and a few close friends.

At first, Michael did not want to think about his illness. "I started drinking a little more to keep from looking at it," he said.[1] But he soon realized that drinking alcohol would not solve his problem. It would only create new ones. He gave up alcohol completely in 1992.

Michael kept on making movies. Taking medicine helped him feel better, and the other actors did not know anything was wrong. But Michael was going through a tough time as an actor. His next few movies, *For Love or Money* (1993), *Life with Mikey* (1993), and *Greedy* (1994), did not become hits.

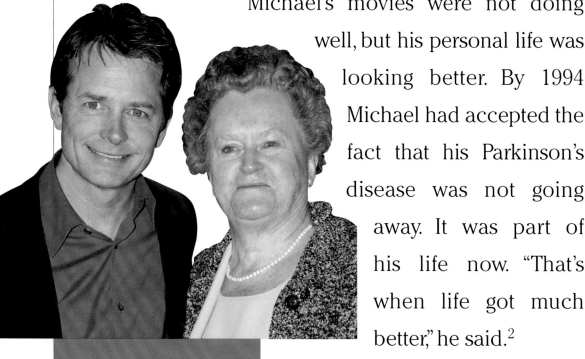

Michael and his mother in 2002.

Michael's movies were not doing well, but his personal life was looking better. By 1994 Michael had accepted the fact that his Parkinson's disease was not going away. It was part of his life now. "That's when life got much better," he said.[2]

Several things helped Michael find the courage to

face his illness. One was understanding more about it. Medicines and new treatments gave him hope. Most of all, Michael knew what was important to him: His family came first.

The Fox family was growing. In 1995, Michael and Tracy celebrated the birth of twin daughters, Aquinnah and Schuyler. Soon after, Michael went to New Zealand for seven months to make a scary movie called *The Frighteners*.

> Michael worked hard to find the courage to face his illness.

Michael hated being across the world from his family. Filming a TV show would not take him so far away from the people he loved. He began looking for a way to get back into television.

Michael helped create a new television series, *Spin City*. The show began in 1996 on ABC-TV. Michael

Graduation Day

Michael was not proud of quitting school. "I don't recommend that to anyone," he said.[3] In 1994 he took a test to earn a special high school diploma called a GED (General Equivalency Diploma).

starred as Mike Flaherty, the deputy mayor of New York City.

For a movie, the actors do their scenes for the camera crew. But *Spin City* was taped in front of an audience. Michael loved that.[4] *Spin City* was a hit from the start. Filming was done in New York City, where the Fox family had lived since 1992. This meant that Michael could be home with his wife and children each night.

For Michael, it was getting harder to keep his Parkinson's disease a secret. He had told the top people at ABC about his illness before he started filming the show. But he did not tell the cast and crew of *Spin City*. The other actors had no idea their star was ill.

When Michael finished filming *Spin City* in March 1998, he told the other actors that he had Parkinson's disease. He also wanted them to know that he was about to have brain surgery.

Michael and Barry Bostwick in *Spin City*.

Michael's family is more important to
him than anything else in his life.

CHAPTER 5

On to the Future

Michael's left arm was shaking so badly that it was making the rest of his body shake, too. After the surgery, his left arm was better.

Then, only a few days later, Michael noticed that his right hand was twitching. "I was sad, but I wasn't angry," he said.[1] It was just one of the many challenges of living with Parkinson's.

Michael was getting tired of keeping such a big secret from his fans. He was ready to let everyone know. Michael told a writer for *People* magazine about his illness. He said that he had been living with Parkinson's for seven years. The magazine came out in November 1998. Next he talked with Barbara Walters on the ABC television show *20/20*.

Michael worried about what people would say. He was amazed at how many letters he got from friends, fans, and other people with Parkinson's disease.[2]

Michael appeared on television with Barbara Walters to tell the world about his life with Parkinson's disease.

Michael won another Emmy, in 2000, for his acting on *Spin City*.

In January 2000, Michael had more surprising news. He said he was leaving *Spin City* at the end of the season. He wanted to spend more time with his family. He was also working hard to fight against Parkinson's disease.

In May 2000, Michael started the Michael J. Fox Foundation for Parkinson's Research. The purpose was to teach people about the disease and to raise money for research.

Michael began to speak out about Parkinson's.

He also became a U.S. citizen. He had been living in the United States for twenty years as a Canadian citizen.

In 2001, the Foxes had another daughter, Esme. It was less than two months after terrorists had crashed airplanes into the World Trade Center in New York City and the Pentagon in Washington, D.C. Many innocent people were killed.

There was so much sadness then. But as Michael held his baby daughter and looked out the hospital window, he felt good about the future. "It was one of those great moments," he said. "Like, the city's going to be OK. We're going to be OK. Life goes on."[3]

Today, much of Michael's time is spent on the work of the Michael J. Fox Foundation. But he is busy in the television and film businesses, too. Now Michael works mostly behind the cameras. That includes doing the voices for characters in movies his children can enjoy.

An actor who speaks for a cartoon character is doing a "voice-over." Michael's first voice-over was in 1993, when he was the voice of Chance the dog in *Homeward Bound: The Incredible Journey*. Since then, he has done voice-overs for Chance in *Homeward Bound II: Lost in San Francisco* (1996), Stuart Little the mouse in the film *Stuart Little* (1999), the explorer Milo in *Atlantis: The Lost Empire* (2001), and Stuart in *Stuart Little 2* (2002).

Michael also turned to writing. *Lucky Man*, a book about his life, was published in 2002. The money he earns from sales of the book goes to his foundation for research on Parkinson's disease. By 2004, the foundation had given more than $42 million to research projects.

For *Stuart Little 2*, Michael posed with an actor dressed as a big mouse.

On December 16,
2002, Michael
was honored
with a star on
the Hollywood
Walk of Fame.

In February 2004, Michael talked to *People* magazine about a new drug he was taking. "It's given me a lot of relief, and I've been able to play hockey, play guitar and do a lot of things I haven't been able to do in a while," he said.[4] He also showed up a couple of times on the NBC television program *Scrubs*.

Parkinson's disease has created problems for Michael, but it has not taken away his joy in everyday pleasures like being with his family. He is proud, too, of the work he does for the Michael J. Fox Foundation. "I'm enjoying life," he says.[5]

Michael faces each day with courage. He helps others

Michael's disease has not stopped him from doing what he loves.

"With both of us in this fight, we're going to win," said Muhammad Ali.[6] The former boxing champ also has Parkinson's disease.

to face the problems in their lives, too. He has great hope for the future. "The war against Parkinson's is a winnable war," he says.[7] Michael plans to be part of that victory.

Timeline

1961   Born on June 9 in Edmonton, Alberta, Canada.

1977   Begins his professional acting career with a role in a Canadian TV series, *Leo and Me*.

1979   Moves to Hollywood to continue his acting career.

1982   Begins playing Alex P. Keaton in the television series *Family Ties*.

1988   Marries actress Tracy Pollan.

1991   Learns that he has Parkinson's disease.

1996   Begins a new television series, *Spin City*.

1998   Tells the world he has Parkinson's disease. Has brain surgery.

2000   Starts the Michael J. Fox Foundation for Parkinson's Research.

2002   *Lucky Man*, a book about his life, is published.

Michael's Movies
A Selected List

Midnight Madness (1980)
Class of 1984 (1982)
High School U.S.A., TV (1983)
Poison Ivy, TV (1985)
Back to the Future (1985)
Teen Wolf (1985)
Light of Day (1987)
Secret of My Success (1987)
Bright Lights, Big City (1988)
Back to the Future II (1989)
Casualties of War (1989)
Back to the Future III (1990)
The Hard Way (1991)
Doc Hollywood (1991)
Homeward Bound: The Incredible Journey, voice (1993)
For Love or Money (1993)
Where the Rivers Flow North (1993)
Life With Mikey (1993)
Don't Drink the Water, TV (1994)
Greedy (1994)
The American President (1995)
Blue in the Face (1995)
Cold Blooded (1995)
The Frighteners (1996)
Mars Attacks! (1996)
Homeward Bound II: Lost in San Francisco, voice (1996)
Stuart Little, voice (1999)
Atlantis: The Lost Empire, voice (2001)
Stuart Little 2, voice (2002)

Back to the Future

Doc Hollywood

Words to Know

cast—The actors in a show are called the "cast." To be "cast" in a show means to be given a part to play.

comedy—A show that is funny and has a happy ending.

drama—A show that is serious.

Emmy Award—Awards that honor television shows and their actors. Emmys are given by a group called the Academy of Television Arts and Sciences.

research—Studying something to learn more about it.

role—The part someone plays in a show.

set—The place where a movie or TV show is filmed.

twitch—A quick movement that a person cannot control.

Chapter Notes

CHAPTER 1.
Too Small for Hockey

1. Susan Granger, "The Clean-cut Kids," *Ladies' Home Journal*, April 1987, p. 181.

2. "Michael J. Fox," *Good Housekeeping*, August 1987, p. 50.

3. "They Like Mike: When Michael J. Fox Calls, Hollywood Answers with $4.5 Million," *People*, December 24, 2001, p. 15.

4. Michael J. Fox, *Lucky Man: A Memoir* (New York: Hyperion Books, 2002), p. 62.

CHAPTER 2.
Rising Star

1. Mark Morrison, "Michael J. Fox Unwinds," *Rolling Stone*, March 12, 1987, p. 52.

CHAPTER 3.
Back to the Future—Again

1. Michael Alexander, "Getting Back to His Future," *People*, December 4, 1989, p. 144.

CHAPTER 4.
A Huge Secret

1. "Oprah Talks to Michael J. Fox and Tracy Pollan," *O, The Oprah Magazine*, March 2002, p. 200.

2. "Oprah Talks" article, p. 201.

Chapter Notes

3. "Michael J. (What a) Fox!" *Teen Magazine*, March 1984, p. 51.

4. Martha Frankel, "The Happiest, Cutest (Ok, and Shortest) Couple in Showbiz," *Redbook*, September 1996, pp. 106+.

CHAPTER 5.
On to the Future

1. Michael J. Fox, *Lucky Man: A Memoir* (New York: Hyperion Books, 2002), p. 210.

2. Patrick Perry, "Michael J. Fox's Challenging New Role," *Saturday Evening Post*, September 2000, p. 38.

3. Brian D. Johnson, "Michael Then and Now: The Former Boy Wonder from B.C. Finds Peace in His Fight Against Parkinson's," *Maclean's*, April 29, 2002, p. 36.

4. "Pop Quiz: Michael J. Fox," *People*, February 23, 2004, p. 26.

5. "Pop Quiz" article, p. 26

6. "State of Grace," *People*, March 25, 2002, p. 111.

7. Steven Reddicliffe, "A Graceful Good-Bye," *TV Guide*, May 13, 2000, p. 74.

Learn More

Books

Bankston, John. *Michael J. Fox: A Real-Life Reader Biography*. Bear, Del.: Mitchell Lane Publishers, 2002.

Vander Hook, Sue. *Parkinson's Disease*. Mankato, Minn.: Smart Apple Media, 2000.

Wheeler, Jill C. *Michael J. Fox*. Edina, Minn.: ABDO Publishing Company, 2001.

Internet Addresses

The official Michael J. Fox fan club.
<http://members.aol.com/FiloFox>

The Michael J. Fox Foundation for Parkinson's Research site. Includes a short biography about Michael, plus information about the foundation and Parkinson's disease.
<http://www.michaeljfox.org>

Index

Pages with photographs are in **boldface** type.